Out of the
ASHES RISES the
Sequoia Tree

Out of the
ASHES RISES the
Sequoia Tree
The Wisdom in Pain

FARANGISS SEDAGHATPOUR

Out of the Ashes Rises the Sequoia Tree

A tribute to my beloved late husband,

Vahid Sedaghatpour

Acknowledgments

To all those who have been pained in life, whatever the reason or circumstance, I acknowledge you.

I acknowledge your trials and tribulations. I acknowledge your fear.

I acknowledge your tears.

I acknowledge your hardship. My heart understands *you*.

I also acknowledge your joy. I acknowledge your success.

I acknowledge your moments of fulfillment. I acknowledge your wisdom and knowing. For all exist within all of us.

I acknowledge *you*.

Contents

Vahid Sedaghatpour was born on December 12, 1956, in Tehran, Iran. He was one of seven children, second to last.

Vahid moved to the United States as a student in 1974 at age eighteen and studied at New York Institute of Technology.

Vahid and I met in September of 1988 and were married six months later. We were blessed with three children.

Vahid was diagnosed with advanced prostate cancer eighteen years into our marriage at the young age of fifty. He navigated through life with this cancer for the next ten years. He left this world at age sixty on June 23, 2017, at 11:17 a.m.

If there was one word for me to describe Vahid, it would be *eccentric*. His personality was eccentric. He had a certain aura about him that was noticeable in any room, any situation, anywhere. His presence was eccentric. He captivated a roomful of crowd with his being, his jokes, his one-of-a-kind dance, and his million-dollar smile.

Vahid's eccentric personality intensified during the last year and a half of his life. As his situation deteriorated, his open heart, his unbounded love, increased by the day.

In his last year, he never ever failed to remind me how beautiful I was to him, how proud he was of our family, and how much he loved the kids and I, and he continuously asked for forgiveness if he hadn't shown his love enough times.

In the last year of his life, the weaker his body became, the more his soul shined through and the greater his light was; and instead of complaining more about the excruciating pain that he was going through, he used his words and energy to compliment the family to express love and gratitude.

On the day of his passing, he had an aura of someone who is complete in his life, having left no loose ends. He left knowing how much he was loved, and he let us know how much he loved us.

This little book is about my soul growth during this time and what I have come to know to be true.

It's about the aspects and dimensions of my inner reservoir and tapping into them at the most painful time of our life.

The pain had many facets. It consisted of the pain of ten years of looking for solutions and healing. It was the pain of fear of the unknown, fear of the future, and fear of facing death. The pain especially intensified the last year of his life, as this handsome, agile tall person who was my partner in life was reduced to being in bed most of the time with pain and no energy.

The pain for me was watching it happen right in front of my eyes with not much control. It was also the pain of watching my children being in this place. The worst of all pains was the pain of losing him.

It's six months after his passing that I'm writing this. The pain has a different texture. There is a void, an emptiness that's indescribable.

And yet I have come to know that love never disappears. It can change form, but love never leaves. Love just is.

I have come to know that the fulfillment of our lives comes through wholeness and how crucial it is to be whole with everything and everyone in our lives.

Wholeness, just like happiness, is not an end unto itself. It's a path to evolve into our highest selves.

I have come to know the power of words spoken and how simple gratitude can set in motion events that become almost miraculous.

This little book is about embracing the pain and allowing it to expand who we are.

Vahid's body has left; however, his presence, his love, and his being that's indefinable are with my family and I every second of the day.

I want to thank Vahid for who he was and continues to be. For to me, his life has not ended.

I'm grateful for our time together and humbled by how he chose to shine through the hardest and final moments of his physical life.

I'm indebted to him for he has shown me, through being who he was, how to continue to lead my life, what's important, what to strive for, and how to be.

As a final note, Vahid was not defined by the disease, sadness, and fears, but rather, *he* defined his life through who he chose to be.

What a gift he was to me, our children, our family, our friends, and the community.

What a gift his love continues to be.

There is a certain wisdom in pain, that if not tapped into, the pain would have been in vain.

Introduction

L ooking at the sequoia tree, you see the miracle of life before you. The tree defies logic by all accounts. It is enormously tall. It's gigantically wide. It seems like it lives forever, with the oldest tree believed to be older than three thousand years old. However, the most intriguing aspect of it is that during forest fires, which can be common in the area of its habitation, its bark does not get consumed by fire. This fact by itself is miraculous on all accounts. Imagine the bark of a tree, which we use to make fire, not being burned down by fire. Not only is it not burned downby fire, but it also uses the fire for its growth and its advantage.

The sequoia tree can do that because of two characteristics it possesses. One is that the bark produces a chemical that's a fire retardant, and two is that the bark is spongelike. It's not compact like other tree barks and retains moisture.

The seed of the sequoia tree might remain dormant for twenty to twenty-five years, until the fire cracks it open. The seed uses the ashes from the fire to germinate.

The sequoia tree stands extremely tall. It can do that because of the roots. The roots of the tree intertwine with one another, causing a network of stability and strength that allows for all the sequoia trees to stand tall. That's why they are always found in groves. They don't grow alone but in communities because it's the roots of one another that allow for such growth upward, defying gravity.

The sequoia tree became my point of reference during the most challenging, fearful time that we went through. It became an imagery of fire, ashes, and a very tall tree being completely unaffected by the chaos that's around it. If anything, it grew even higher because of it.

The image gave me point of reference that if it's possible for a tree to not only survive fire but also thrive through the fire, it *must* be possible for any human being to not only survive darkness, sadness, and challenge but also thrive from it.

Everything we see and observe in this world is a reflection of who we are, what we are capable of, and what is possible.

As we look at the sequoia tree, what becomes possible for us? How can we not be consumed by the fires of our lives? How can we use the fire and its ashes to grow from the experience? What ingredient(s) do we need to have our bark, our core, be fire-resistant? How can we defy gravity and, despite of it, grow tall?

To ask the questions differently, what are the ingredients that allow us to thrive through the fire of our lives, that allow us to rise out of the ashes as a giant and master of character?

What quality in us can be compared to the fire retardant in the bark of the tree? What quality is the fire retardant?

Each one of us has the ability to rise out of the ashes of our lives and become the pillar of stability, strength, and support. Only we can tap into our own inner reservoir. Only we are able to invoke the power of the fire retardant that lies within each one of us.

Through the pain of everything my husband and I went through, I have come to know certain truths.

I have come to know that we too, just like the sequoia tree, have fire retardants. I have come to know that there are hidden qualities that we each possess that germinate through the challenges of our lives, just like the sequoia seed.

I have come to know the power of choosing to develop these inner qualities and how it can enhance not only our lives but also the lives of others.

These truths are as follows:

1. Life as a journey
2. Divine providence
3. Surrender
4. Faith
5. Gratitude
6. Love
7. Wholesomeness
8. Family/friends/community

This is my knowing, my truths. It is true for me.

In sharing, maybe it opens a pathway for you that will allow you to come to your own knowing. Knowing is different from reading a book or hearing it from someone we consider a teacher. It is to know with every cell of your body that it is true.

It's yours, and no one, no circumstance, no pain, no situation can take that knowing away from you.

By sharing, I hope you resonate with some points, if not all, and you find that inner beauty and peace within all the seeming pain and chaos that you might be going through or have gone through in the past.

I pray that no one has to go through pain to come to a certain knowing and truth. However, there is a certain wisdom in pain that if not tapped into, then the pain would have been in vain. The wisdom is like the sequoia seed that opens through fire and germinates from the ashes. Wisdom becomes revealed through these times, which, if allowed, can germinate in the hardest of all times and, with the right ingredients of love and nurture, become a foundation for our soulful selves.

At the very least, we need to look beyond the suffering and glance at the light that sits embedded within the pain.

In reading the book, I ask that you don't believe anything I say but, rather, feel and see what resonates with you and your soul.

I ask that you be open and allow things to find its own way to your heart and place of knowing.

Pain has many different facets and dimensions, and I came to know many of them especially in the last year and a half of my husband's life. The pain at times was so intense that my internal organs, which I'm usually unaware of, would start hurting. Don't let anyone tell you that the pain is an illusion. It's very real, as real as joy, as tangible as an object, as intense as a hurricane. Don't let anyone tell you how to feel and how to be, for to me, that's the most inhumane thing we can do: to rob someone of their emotions and tell them that for certain reasons that we think, they should feel differently.

Pain is real, just like fire is real. Pain hurts, just like fire burns. Pain can wreak havoc in one's life, just like fire can wreak havoc.

Having said all that, there are internal gifts that we all possess that can allow us to not get consumed by the fire. The pain breaks it open and brings it to the surface, bringing out the wisdom that's inherent in all our souls.

We can deepen our roots during these painful times, we can stimulate the fire retardant in our bark, we can draw moisture into our bark, we can use the ashes to grow, we can intertwine with other roots for support, and ultimately, we can grow through the pain, becoming taller in height, deeper in roots.

The first few chapters are what allows us to deepen our roots. The next chapters are what I believe to be the fire retardant in our being that, if we chose to, can get released.

Unfortunately, I cannot speak for Vahid. He would have had much wisdom to share. I can only share what I experienced through how he was being, some of which I will share in different parts of the book. However, I do know that Vahid's presence grew ever stronger with each passing day through the smoke and fire of his life and he left this world as a giant of a being.

Each one of us has the ability
to rise out of the ashes of our
lives and become the pillar of
stability, strength, and support.

Journey

The journey is a journey of light, transcendence, love, wholeness, completeness, and interconnectedness.

I t's all about the journey of our soul both individually and as it relates to the bigger tapestry of creation.

We are all on a journey.

The journey is a journey of light, transcendence, love, wholeness, completeness, and interconnectedness.

It's about the evolvement of our souls and the experiences we need to have in order to have the awakening of Divine perfection and order.

It's a journey of consciousness and giving permission for the greater consciousness to fill our lives. We, in our limited vision, have no way of knowing where along this path of awakening we are. However, it's to know that the universe is always expanding and evolving and that we too, no matter what it seems from the outside and no matter what the circumstances are, if we allow ourselves, are also expanding.

We tend to give the points, or certain stops in our journey, a name, judging that point in time as good or bad, and yet in the bigger picture, in the wider perspective, it's neither good nor bad, just an experience that has the potential to bring us to greater awareness if we choose to.

Everything, every experience, every inspiration, every seeming failure, every fall, every circumstance is to bring us to that expansive place of knowing.

On this journey, nothing ever goes unnoticed, or nothing ever gets lost. There are no thoughts, words, or actions that get vaporized into thin air. Every goodness, love, joy, connection and—on the other end of the spectrum—guilt, resentment, shame, blame, fear, and hate stays on this journey, till the time and awareness come that all the latter be transformed into the former.

Throughout the days when my dear husband was in pain, going through chemo, ending up in emergency rooms faster than I could spell out our last name, many people with the best of intentions would say, "You don't deserve this. Your husband is so kind. He doesn't deserve this."

On this journey we call life, I have come to know that there is no such thing as *deserve*. By saying that one doesn't deserve the circumstances that one has been handed with, are we suggesting that somebody else might deserve such circumstances?

No one deserves such pain and suffering, *no one.*

I also came to know that I must let go of what I think we deserve or what I think our lives should have / could have looked like, for that would bring me much suffering.

Suffering and pain are two separate entities. We tend to use the words simultaneously; however, they are very different in their content.

Pain is pain, and there are many facets to pain. Suffering, on the other hand, is resistance to the circumstances of our lives as it's happening in real time.

Suffering is when we say this should not be so. My life should be different. I don't deserve this. Suffering takes us away from the moment, from attention to the moment, and from what needs to be done at the moment.

Once I was able to distinguish between pain and suffering, I was able to let go of *deserve, should be, why is it* and be accepting of the pain at hand and yet not suffer.

The word *deserve* acts on the "poor me" version. The "poor me" has limited access to being present as life is happening and evolving. The "poor me" does not allow us to be present for what needs to be done today with love.

Once I was able to know that life is a journey as Truth, with many stops that are neither good nor bad, I was able to ask, what do I need to do today? How may I be present for Vahid today?

Fast-forward to today, how may I be present to my life? How may I be present to my children?

It's not to say that I have no pain. It's to say that I'm not suffering through the pain. I'm not being consumed by the pain. I'm in pain yet present.

Resisting our journey, avoiding the ups and downs of our path, makes us fall into a bottomless pit in which the only salvation out is by accepting our journey as it's evolving and showing itself every day at every moment.

One day, in the midst of all the challenges, I decided I need to walk it off. I needed fresh air and the serenity of nature to embrace me. So I went for a hike.

As I was on this hike, I understood what "journey" of our lives really means. It's almost as if the mountain, the path that I had taken, was speaking to me.

On that day, these are the things I learned from hiking on the mountain:

1. The mountain that I was hiking on was a result of a volcanic eruption many thousand years ago, yet the land was extremely fertile with not only magnificent trees but also vineyards and farmland on top of the mountain. I realized, in our lives, when we have an eruption, if we are patient, it can serve as a conduit for growth and fertility for generations to come.

2. The walk had many ups and downs, some of which were challenging for me to climb, and on the downs, I was scared of slipping because it was too steep. I couldn't really label the up as bad just because it was too challenging for me, nor could I say that the steepness was bad. It was just a path and needed to be walked to get to destination. It's just like life. Neither the down nor the up is considered as bad or good. It's a path of our lives and must be traveled.

3. I wasn't wearing proper sneakers, and therefore, my walk was slower than others. In life, it's important to have the right gears or the right tools for our journey. It makes the walk to our destination much more enjoyable.

4. It's about enjoying the view, taking in the beauty while you are on the path, while you are on the journey. It's taking in the moment as each step forward brings with it.

5. As I passed each curve, it brought with it a different view, some of them magnificent and breathtaking. As I was on the curve, I had no idea what's to come and had a very limited view. In life, there are many times when we are on the curve, when we don't have access to a wide view, or when our vision is limited to the curve. If we are patient, just around the corner might be the most beautiful moments of our lives.

6. The destination is important; otherwise, you can get lost in the ups and downs of life. Either the up will define you or the down. It's easy to be defined and be confused by the path, rather than being defined by our own agility, strength, and willingness to move forward, in the face of the hardship of the path, and not give up walking.

7. Every step builds the stamina for the next, if we don't allow ourselves to be defined, have a vision, and are equipped.

8. The less baggage we carry on our backs on our journey, the more agile we are and the less tired we get. The baggage on our backs is the heaviness that we carry from the past, the so-called failures, the misjudgments, the hurt, and the pain. We can, if we choose to, put down the bag gently, thank it, and continue on our journey.

9. There were a few times when the height was too high for me to hike on, especially that I didn't have the right shoes and I stayed behind the group. One person from the group came back for me and said, "Do you need a helping hand?" At that moment, I burst into tears. I said, "Yes, I need a helping hand." I needed a helping hand not only on that hike but also in my journey at that moment in time. I realized that when you have a helping hand at times when you are too tired and feel like you can't go on anymore, it makes you move rather than being stuck in that place of "I can't do it anymore." We also have to be willing to say that we need a helping hand at that moment in time and be able to receive the support.

So the path taught me about patience—patience through the fire and eruption of our lives. It might be, it might just be, that if we are patient, we can transform our lives from a volcano to a majestic mountain that is extremely fertile. It's like the sequoia tree that uses fire and ash to grow higher and stronger. It needs patience.

We need the right tools. These are our internal tools that we are going to explore in the book.

We can, if we choose to, drop our baggage and journey in our lives lighter and with more agility, remember not to be defined by any particular ups or downs of our lives and not to be defined by our success or our failures. It's just our path.

As we travel the path, the word *deserve* has no longer any meaning because it's just a path.

The path has the potential to build my stamina, my strength, my patience, my faith that, around the corner, might be the most magnificent thing that I have ever witnessed: persistence of just walking toward the destination and trusting that even if you can't walk up or down because of steepness, there is help and you will get there.

In closing, life is a journey. Don't allow yourself to be the victim of the ups and downs of life. It's a path that must be walked on. You and only you can walk your path. No one else can walk the path for you. We can get help, we can get a helping hand, but ultimately, only we can walk the path.

One possible phrase to say to oneself is this: "Life is a journey. I allow for its evolvement and unfoldment. I am present to the call of my journey."

Surrender

Surrender is active, alive, with knowledge and choice.

I always had a hard time with the concept of surrender, and yes, it was a concept for me, till my husband fell really ill.

I only came to know surrender then and only then.

At some point, things had gotten so intense that I had lost control of everything. I couldn't make any decisions, even small ones such as making dinner, since at any given moment, we might end up in the emergency room.

What I learned at some point was to say that I give up knowing how and what the future should look like and yet be ever so present to the call of the moment.

The choices that I ended up making were literally from moment to moment.

Surrender might sound as inaction, giving up, passivity, and yet surrender is active, alive, with knowledge and choice.

Surrender allowed me to put my energy in the moment rather than wasting my precious mental and emotional energy on the fear of the future or events of the past.

The act of surrender allowed me to be more present with my husband, present with his needs, and most important, present and alive with his love.

Surrender is a moment-to-moment decision. It is not a onetime choice but a lifelong choice to let go of the face of the future and the fears associated with it and to let go of the notion of how things should have been versus how things are.

Surrender is embracing the moment as it's happening and surrendering to a greater purpose that the Divine has for us.

It's surrendering to the big picture and knowing that the tapestry of my life is being woven from minute to minute, and there is no way for me to know that this particular thread that is weaving my life right now is right or wrong, good or bad, since I can't see the bigger form of the tapestry.

Surrender is being receptive to the good that is around us. It is the act of embracing the beauty that's in our lives as well as our challenges.

One of the great things that bring us great suffering, causing much anxiety and fear, is the attempt to will things to be different from what we are presented with.

Don't get me wrong, we must have action. However, we can't control many things, especially the outcome of that which we try.

We have to do what we can.

I, in my fullest capacity, did what I could for my husband. We went to the best doctors, got the best treatments, went on a macrobiotic diet, did visualizations, did meditation, and prayed. The surrender came when I was able to let go of the fear of the outcome and just allow life to present itself as it does.

Let life do life, and I do love. In that surrender, I found peace.

Surrender gives us the possibility of living in possibility. Anything is possible. Healing is possible. Joy is possible. Dancing with life is possible rather than resisting the lives we have. Appreciation is possible. Love is possible. All becomes possible no matter what the circumstances are presenting themselves as.

Surrender gives us the possibility of surrendering to the bigger dream that life has for us, surrendering the dream to the bigger Divine flow that is our life.

When there is a fire, the sequoia tree doesn't fold itself and become small. Rather, it activates its internal fire retardant to not be consumed by fire. Once the fire subsides, it uses the ashes as fertilizer for its growth.

One of our internal fire retardants is surrender. Let fire be fire. Let it burn the extra bushes and weeds that inhibit the growth of the sequoia tree because it takes away from its nutrition. Let fire do what fire does. Let our challenges be our challenges. Let our pain be our pain. However, let us not be burned from the fire. Let us invoke and bring out the sequoia tree within us and use the fire to grow through the challenge, to not be consumed by the challenge. Use the challenge to break open seeds of wisdom that can germinate in the ashes. The breaking open of the seed and its germination need surrender, not resistance.

Imagine the seed resisting to break open. Imagine the seed consciously saying, "I'm breaking apart, I'm disintegrating, I will resist this to my last breath." What is the seed giving up? By resisting, it's giving up being a majestic tree. It's in its surrender that allows for disintegration, germination, and growth of the tree.

Surrender is to get out of our own way, to allow, to accept, and simply be present to the call of the moment.

One phrase that one could use is this: "I surrender to the possibilities of love and healing."

Divine providence

G-d is above creation,
yet he is within creation.
There is no place that's void
of him, not even in pain.

This is true for me. I hope some part or all of it resonates with you.

G-d is here, right now.

He is aware of my going and my coming. Not only is He aware, but His infinite knowledge also guides my going and coming.

It's not to say that I don't have freedom of choice, for that is the greatest gift that G-d has given to mankind.

The guidance of G-d in my life could be contradictory to having freedom of choice, but it's not to me.

G-d is found not only in holy places as we deem to be holy but also in every place and every moment. He cares about every mundane aspect of my life. Only G-d is aware of the full spectrum of my journey and knows where on this path of evolvement I am.

Only G-d, in His infinite wisdom, knows what situations, what circumstances, and who and what needs to appear in my life in order to assist me to evolve into who I need to be.

G-d is above creation, yet He is within creation.

It is said that G-d Himself visits the sick. He doesn't send His angels or messengers. He himself comes upon the person who is suffering.

G-d is not only found in the perfection of nature or the perfect human being, but He is also present with the sick, unable, incapable, suffering souls. He Himself gives them the strength to be and to endure what they are enduring.

G-d is intimate with His creation, especially with human beings who are here for a purpose and mission, each on our own unique journey.

G-d is especially intimate with those who allow Him in even while going through very challenging and dark periods.

G-d desires an intimate relationship with human beings. However, intimacy can only come if we desire it and if we allow for it. By starting this desire for intimacy, we allow for partnership with the Divine.

Becoming partners means that we are a channel for His light and love to move through us no matter what the circumstances present themselves as.

Becoming partners means that we are willing to give up suffering, giving it over to G-d and allowing Him to handle the situation.

By giving up suffering, I don't mean there is no pain. Giving up suffering means that we are willing to give up the questions "Why?" "Why me?" and "Why would G-d do this to me?"

If we are able to let go of the questions that we really have no answers for and instead allow G-d to take over, not only does it bring greater peace, but it also allows us to be present for possibilities to flow through—possibilities of peace, serenity, calmness, knowingness, and connection.

We can be in pain but not in suffering, we can be in the dark but not be lost, we can be in a challenge but not be in a struggle, we can be in fire but not be consumed—by allowing G-d in.

G-d is in dark and light.

There is no place that's void of Him, *no place*.

The only place that has the possibility of being void of Him is our hearts. If we close our hearts to Him, He is unable to make a partnership with us, let alone an intimate relationship.

In this partnership, we trust that by handing it to G-d, we will be given the best possible situation as G-d sees fit in the bigger picture.

The start of this intimacy is seeing Divine providence in all that is.

Faith

Faith is a choice. It's a moment to moment conscious choice.

Faith is a state of the soul. It's part of the Divine. It is what the soul inherits, even if we question, even if we ask why, even if we are angry. It's inherent and remains uncompromised even if it's untapped.

And yet faith is a choice. It's a moment-to-moment conscious choice.

In the choice of the moment to connect to our soul's inherent quality of faith, fear in that moment becomes nonexistent.

We oscillate between faith and fear at all times. If left unchecked, we can live in fear most of the time, if not all the time. It is when we are aware, that we can extract out the hidden faith part of ourselves and live in that space.

Faith and fear cannot coexist in the same moment. It's either-or.

Fear shows itself in many different ways, with many different facets and colorations to the extent that it's sometimes unrecognizable.

Fear in and of itself is not necessarily a bad thing. Fear has served as a way of survival for human beings for millennia. Fear alerts us and makes us watch out, watch our back, watch our surroundings, watch stepping into the future. In a way, it has served us well.

The problem with fear is that any challenge to the existing status quo is seen as a threat. Any disturbance in our mind's eye about our future is perceived as the enemy. Even though this is perceptual and there is no actual threat, our reactions are similar to that of being attacked at this moment.

Fear in the face of challenge is absolutely normal, and that's our first reaction. However, to rise above the fear, to transcend the fear, to go through the challenge without being compromised, to not be consumed by fear, we need *faith*.

Faith is the fire retardant that the sequoia tree produces during a fire. Faith is the invisible spiritual substance that we produce, as a choice, day by day, to not be burned through the pain and challenge that we might be facing.

The sequoia tree not only is not burned through it, but uses the ashes from other shrubs and trees burned, as fertilizer.

Faith will not only contain us and protect us from falling into despair, sadness, and darkness, but once the fire is set off, it will use the remnants of the challenge to become wisdom that will feed our souls and allow us to deepen our roots and grow taller than before the fire started.

Fear is neither good nor bad and should not be named as such. Of course, we have fear. It's part of our humanity. It has served us at times, and it will continue to serve us to a certain degree. It is when fear becomes the strong voice and paralyzes us that it becomes a culprit in our growth.

Once we recognize fear, we can choose faith. Again, it's a moment-to-moment choice because that recognition is in the moment.

Fear has many facets. I can share with you some of my fears within the ten years that my husband was diagnosed and all the emotional turmoil that we went through. (In here, I can only speak of my own fears, not my husband's.)

These were some of my fears, and maybe you can recognize some of your own fears. I ask that we not label any of our fears as good or bad, only to recognize that it's there:

- What will happen to my husband?
- Are we heading for disaster?
- What will happen to my kids?
- How can I manage?
- I can't manage if anything happened to him.
- I can't deal with this.
- We are doomed for a major crash in our lives.
- What will happen to our livelihood?
- What will happen when the pillar of our lives is no longer here?
- I will be paralyzed.
- I won't be able to breathe if anything happens to my husband.
- I can't bear to lose him.
- Losing Vahid will be devastating to our family.

At times, the very fear of the future and its consequences did paralyze me. I did fall on my face with fear many times.

However, I was blessed to have teachers in my life who reminded me to connect to the faith within. With their love, compassion, and care, they guided me to tap to the inner knowing and connect to G-d's love and

His blueprint for our lives. They guided me to trust the blueprint, let go of fear, and have faith in how things unfold.

With their support and love, I was able to choose the path of faith.

It was and still is a moment-to-moment decision.

What faith has allowed me to do is to enjoy the moment with my husband throughout the ten years of disease, as well as our children as they were growing up; otherwise, I would have lost all the joyous moments, being seeped in sadness and pain.

I decided to give the future to G-d and instead be fully present in the moment with my children and husband.

It gave me the opportunity to make decisions that were based on knowledge rather than fear. It allowed me to laugh and bring joy in the home.

It allowed me to create a space of love and togetherness in my home.

In the face of fear, none of that would have existed.

How do we tap into this faith?

The first of the Ten Commandments is a statement and not a commandment. The statement can read as, "I am G-d who takes you out of darkness and challenge."

The first commandment is a statement of Faith. G-d is saying, "Believe in me that I am the one and the only one who takes you out of a narrow place in your life."

This is the foundation, to believe and know that G-d is a personal G-d who not only has created heaven and earth but is also a G-d who cares about my affairs, my well-being and that He is the one who can bring me out of any challenge no matter how impossible it might seem to me.

This is passive faith, where I need to consciously work on recognizing G-d in my life and have faith that only good can come from it all.

In another account in the Torah, the Jewish Holy Bible, when the Israelites were leaving to go to the Promised Land, they encountered the sea. They had no way back, as the army was pursuing them, with no way to the sides and no way forward, as it was the sea in front of them.

Most of us are under the impression that at this point Moses lifted up his cane and the sea opened. However, something crucial happened before this event.

One man out of hundreds and thousands decided that if G-d had brought them to this place, G-d would also take them out of this place. This man started walking into the sea. He moved in knee-deep water; nothing happened. He moved in shoulder-deep water; nothing happened. He went in neck-deep water; that was when the sea started splitting.

This one man took the faith that was passive and just a belief up to that point and brought it into action. He walked his faith into the sea.

That is the second part of faith, to take faith-based action. When we do that, what seems absolutely impossible has the potential to yield to miracles.

We have to walk our faith even if it seems we are going to drown.

Just walk it.

First part is "G-d will take me out of this challenge." Second part is "I need to walk through it in order that G-d not only takes me out but also shows me His miracles."

The first part for Vahid and I was to know that G-d is with us every step of the way and guiding us, and the second part was to walk that belief, to seek the best doctors and care and also to celebrate life, laugh, and connect with family and friends.

I have been a witness to many miracles in my life. Many things came together at the right time that without G-d's hand would have been impossible.

To this day, I see the miracles working their way in my life and my children's lives.

I know without a shadow of doubt that G-d has our back, that He is protecting us, that He is guiding us to the best possible outcome, and that He is pouring His love for us every second of every day.

This faith has allowed me not to be burned up by the extensive challenges of my life. It has allowed me to have love in my home and in my heart, instead of resentment and anger, for it is so easy to close the heart when we are hurt and in pain.

Faith has allowed me to know that all is well, no matter how the circumstances are presenting themselves.

I have had to make choices, but I have had to also walk those choices.

It is this faith that has given me the gift of no regrets.

Because of this faith, I was able to be present for my husband with all my heart and soul. I was able to share myself with him with love and surround him with love of family.

Had I not done that, I would have always regretted not being there enough for him or not having done enough for him.

With this faith, I was able to give him my 110 percent, without bringing fear to him or to our lives.

It is important throughout our journey in times of crisis and challenge to strengthen not only our faith in the Divine but also our faith in ourselves, to know that if we have been brought to it, we are fully capable of going through it, and to fully know that G-d Himself has faith in us and knows that we can travel through this challenging time without being consumed by fire.

It is also to have faith in the evolvement of life and knowing that even if things look dark from our vantage point, G-d has our back, that life has our back. It is to have faith in life and faith in love.

It is also to have faith in our mission and purpose. To have faith in that is to know, that things have evolved in alignment with our purpose and things will continue to evolve in order to accomplish that which we are here to do. Each one of us is part of the tapestry of the bigger whole, each one of us with our own unique imprints on life.

Everything, all circumstances, and situations are in sync with that purpose even though, from where I'm standing, it doesn't look so.

Faith is also the ability to see our lives from a bird's-eye view rather than from an ant's-eye view. If we are able to look at our lives from a bird's-eye view, we would be seeing a beautiful tapestry that continues to be weaved, and the shape, contours, design, and fabric only come together from that view.

It is to have faith that all is well.

All is with a Divine design.

All is in alignment with a higher purpose.

All is in the right time, right place.

Love

Love is the space that's quiet,
silent, humble, and holy.

I n this journey, I have come to know love—love that is beyond time and space, love that is beyond any circumstance, shape, or form. I have come to know of the timelessness of love and to know that it is always there; we just have to be open to it.

I have come to know that love never fades. If anything, it grows and expands.

I have come to know love and experience love in a greater depth and wider clarity than I ever have, especially during the last year of Vahid's life. I can even go so far as to say that Vahid's experience or, rather, knowing of love completely shifted in the last year of his life. The way he cherished every interaction and gave permission to himself to receive the love was magical. He embraced everyone, embraced every situation, and had loving, meaningful insights that he shared with much compassion and humility. He came to under-stand everyone, where they came from, why they were hurting, and what could be possible for them if they took a different path. It was as though his awareness had expanded with what we get to call love.

I have come to know love as a state of being rather than an experience.

This love is sacred love.

I really believe that we don't have the word, the proper language, to describe the love that transcends it all yet permeates through every aspect of our lives. The only word we have is *love*. This love is beyond feeling, beyond any thought. It's the space that's quiet, silent, humble, and holy. It has no agenda. It binds everything, even the seeming opposites.

This love that I have come to know is the binder that brings all aspects of life together. There is no isolation among any part of life, no isolation between the good and the so- called bad moments of life. There is no separation between the challenging part and the serene part. It is all in unison, as one song, as one tapestry. This love has no agenda except love itself. It knows no boundaries. All boundaries fade away.

Love is like music that has many different notes, but all the notes are part of the beautiful song we call life.

Vahid and I both came to appreciate the different notes and, through this love, were able to bring all aspects of our life together.

Love is always there; however, it needs awareness—the awareness that at any given moment, in any situation, this love can be tapped into, whether it's on a beautiful sunny day by the shores of the ocean or whether it's in the hallways of the emergency room. Love is beyond all that, yet it is within all of it. Vahid's loving awareness never subsided even in the days that he would spend in hospital rooms. He gave his love to the doctors, nurses, other patients in the room, and all were mesmerized by his kindness. He would console the other patients, giving them positive ways to look at their diseases. He would make them laugh with his jokes. He would transform the room with his smile. His love never subsided; it only grew stronger and more tangible.

Vahid's shift in perception allowed him to tap into a deeper love beyond anything he had experienced before. This love gave him the clarity he needed to be whole and complete in his life. This allowed him to forgive many situations and people that had caused him pain and sorrow throughout his life. He forgave all situations and forgave everyone whom he had thought had wronged him or his family one way or another.

When Vahid left this physical world, his whole being was filled with this essence we call love. He was complete in his life, having no regrets and having no anger and resentment about anything or anyone, including his disease.

It is this love that is eternal and knows no time and space.

Vahid's life became the embodiment of loving awareness that he possessed throughout the last year of his life.

There is nothing greater than this love. It is what feeds the soul, what allows us to go through the hardest times not as a failure but as an awakened soul. It is the glue in every aspect of our lives, be it with other people, family, or ourselves.

This love allows us to embrace the pain with dignity. It allows us to navigate through any difficulty and hardship with grace.

On the days that I felt I no longer have it in me to go on, one of the things that allowed me to go through the day with commitment was love—the love for Vahid, the love for my kids, and also the love that Vahid and I received from family and friends.

Please never think that any act of love or kindness is minimal and doesn't mean anything. Every act of kindness, every expression of love, every word that gets uttered becomes part of the fabric of the soul of the person who is in the dark. No matter how small it may seem to your eyes, to the person who is in darkness, with challenge and hardship, that act of love becomes a lit match that can carry them through the day.

I know. I was there.

I also know how Vahid's face would change and brighten up with every act of kindness.

The love that is transcendent is also universal. It's found in the morning breeze, in the flight of a bird, in the changing of seasons, in the sunrise, in the sunset, and in the moonlight.

During the last year of Vahid's life, our awareness of this love became deeper and deeper. We noticed things that went unnoticed before. We both realized that there are gifts within every moment, and our urgency to tap into the love of the moment grew greater with each passing day.

This love allowed both of us to move past regrets, anger for dreams unfulfilled, and resentment toward what was happening and deepened our appreciation for each other and our life as it showed up.

This love allowed us to see from a higher vantage point and have an inclusive attitude about all life. There are no aspects of life that don't belong here. Everything is part of the whole.

It is love that brings healing to the brokenness and the darkness that can at times engulf the soul.

If love could be compared to any part of the sequoia tree, it would be the bark itself, the bark that's wood but doesn't burn through fire, the bark that connects the roots and leaves. If the roots are faith and surrender, the leaves are our action that can give birth to new creation. Love binds the past and the future. It binds the seen and the unseen. It binds the faith in darkness to creativity with awareness.

Love is the bark that stands tall and grows with the challenge and turmoil. It is the bark that defies gravity.

Only love can defy gravity. It is only love that can break through barriers. As a matter of fact, there are no barriers to love.

It is possible to have a life filled with this thing we call love, a love that's boundless, timeless, and effortless, with much humility and serenity.

It is possible. I know.

Gratitude

Gratitude replenishes the darkness
with vitality and flow of life

There are times in our lives that we feel our lives have been reduced to ashes. It feels like all is hopeless, all is for nothing, and there is nothing left to salvage.

Just like ashes that have no life or potential for life, it is good for nothing, not even heat. It is already burned up with no advantage to its existence. Sometimes, it feels like that through the difficulties of life.

And yet it's from the ashes that the seed of the sequoia tree breaks open. It is the ashes that the seed uses to germinate.

The breaking point of the seed in the ashes of our lives is gratitude. The seed could be a seed of wisdom, seed of joy, seed of humility, or seed of light.

Gratitude is the acknowledgment of something or someone in existence. By being grateful for the existence of the person or a thing, we are validating its existence and breathing new life into its being.

Gratitude brings in a new life force into the person or thing that we are acknowledging and replenishes the darkness with vitality and flow of life.

When we are grateful, we are saying thank you for being here right now, at this moment, and we are affirming exchange of energies between the two entities.

Acknowledgment of what already is, as well as giving thanks to it, allows for cocreation, allows for germination of love and appreciation to flow through. It is the ray of light through the storm of life.

It is the germination of goodness in the ashes of our lives.

During the last months of Vahid's physical life, the ingredient that breathed life to him on a daily basis was love, and what brought forth vitality of being was gratitude.

The acknowledgment that the children and I had for him, the acknowledgment of his being, the acknowledgment of his presence, making that alive for him, gave him the opening he needed to embrace the day, even if it felt like ashes.

It was important for us to acknowledge him and his presence, especially in the weakened state that he was in, because he got to express a few times how disappointed he was at the way things had turned out: What would be his purpose for living? If he couldn't work, if he couldn't be active—if, if, if—then what is he good for?

He got to know that we appreciate *him*.

We appreciate and acknowledge his presence.

We acknowledge his being.

We are grateful for his love.

We appreciate everything that he is and stands for, even if he was fragile, weak, and in pain.

He got to know till his last breath how grateful we are to have had a person like that in our lives. It gave him a reason to be, just to be.

That gratitude was expressed not only by us but also by all the family members and friends.

Being grateful is like bringing a bit of heaven down to earth. That's what it was for Vahid. A bit of heaven was brought down for him through all the people that cared for him, and in turn, he gave us a bit of heaven by the serenity and wisdom that came through him. He cracked open the seed of goodness in the ashes of his life, and the access was acknowledgment of his being.

Gratitude is a conscious choice. There are two parts to being grateful: one is to bring our awareness that this is what we are appreciative of; second is to actually say it, whether to G-d, to another person, to ourselves, or to the universe at large. When we do that, we bring a piece of heaven to the darkest place in our lives. This is when germination can take place, the germination of the soul shining through the ashes of our lives.

Gratitude increases our resiliency and our buoyancy so we don't swing from one end of the spectrum to another as circumstances of our lives change.

Change is inevitable. Change is seen in seasons, in the flow of day and night, through the migration of birds, and through the waning and waxing of the moon. Change is inevitable. It is how we go through the change that allows for the deepest reservoirs of our souls to show themselves.

To go through any change in our lives, resilience and buoyancy are key. Gratitude makes the way open and makes it possible for us to stay grounded. Gratitude opens our vision to a wider spectrum of our lives. It allows us to be resilient to the heat and fire that's surrounding us and be buoyant enough to bounce right back even if we feel like there is nowhere to go.

It allows us not to be focused on one aspect of our lives but to be able to see the different colors rather than being stuck on one color in our lives—namely, our challenge—and be able to see the rainbow in our lives and have a sense of appreciation for its highs and lows.

Gratitude allows us to take the focus away from the faults, mistakes, and lack of our lives and put the attention on what's good, what's beautiful, and what's whole just as is.

There is much scientific evidence about practicing gratitude on a daily basis, all well and true. Greater than that is the gift of connection, through acknowledgment and appreciation. If all things fade away in life, one thing that never ever fades away is the strength of connection—the bond that we have made between G-d, ourselves, the others, circumstances, and life. This connection never disappears even after death. It has even the possibility of being strengthened.

Whole and Complete

Being whole is being complete.
It encompasses love, joy, humility,
being one with life, being
one with all there is.

Life seems to be one point after another with no seeming flow between the points. There seems to be a separation and staggered aspect in the moments of our lives. There are also points that look broken, and we say to ourselves these should have never been, these should have never happened, and because of these points, we say, "My life is broken. I am broken." We carry these broken parts in our lives and apply it even to the parts that at the moment are beautiful.

There is another way of being. Life is not separated, but rather, it's a flow. Our lives might have pain, but we are not broken.

The sequoia tree doesn't identify itself with the fire, nor does it identify itself with the smoke and ashes. It doesn't make the fire the culprit of its growth. It keeps going. It keeps evolving. It keeps becoming.

There is another way of being.

I had never in my life, through all the ups and downs, through all my learning and my journey, come to know about a state of being called wholesomeness.

Being whole is being complete. It encompasses love, joy, humility, being one with life, being one with all there is.

I only came to know this state and resided in it through the last weeks of Vahid's life.

This state of being is not talked about much. We talk about love, joy, peace, and serenity but not much about being wholesome. I'm not sure why. I have experienced this to be the highest state of being.

Being whole and complete with our lives gives us the possibility of being good with everything that has happened in our life, with everyone who has showed up in our lives, with the way they have presented themselves and aligning all our life events to the purpose for which we are here on this physical earth.

In wholeness, there is profound and complete forgiveness of all things, people, situations, including ourselves.

It is through Vahid, with the way he presented himself in the last year of his life, that I came to realize that we both had the blessing of entering into a state of being called wholeness.

In that state, there was pure love, there was sacredness to the moment, there was truth. The truth of who he was shone through. There was peace and serenity. All this happened because Vahid came to a place of wholeness in his life, accepting all that was and all that had come to be.

This is the greatest state of being for it's all-encompassing.

He endowed us with a gift before passing, the gift of being whole and complete.

He has given me the awareness to look within my life and be complete with all that was and with everyone who have showed up as they have showed up.

He gave me the awareness that rather than spending time in the past to try to figure out the lack in life, I needed to be, to evolve, to become, and to be peaceful with all that has come to be.

In this state, there is no separation among the parts. There is no sense of brokenness. There is no holding on to memories that hinder our growth.

Wholesomeness needs no thing, needs no title, and needs no status. It's a state of being that has clarity, luminosity, serenity, and connectedness. It's the emergence of the soul outwardly.

To be wholesome is to be in sync with the seed disintegrating in the ashes in order to germinate. It is to allow the flow of life. It is to allow change.

It is to not deny that fire is raging in the forest and to acknowledge the pain, hurt, sadness, and darkness. It is to embrace it all, all of it—the pain with joy, the hurt with moments of clarity, the sadness with moments of fulfillment. It's to embrace it all.

I can't tell you how to be whole, but I can tell you how Vahid and I were able to reach this state.

It's to forgive all events, all people, all situations as they have happened and shown up.

It's to bless all the moments and give thanks for all that has been, even the pain, sadness, and darkness.

It's to unify all points of our lives with love and allow love to fill in the spaces that are void, empty, and broken.

It is to be grateful for all that has been. I know this might sound ridiculous. How can I be grateful for my husband's death? It is because I am grateful for his life, I am grateful for all the moments together, I am grateful for our three children, I am grateful for who he was, I am grateful that I had the privilege of being with him for twenty-eight years.

It is to have faith that from this vantage point, I can't possibly know why things have turned out the way they have, but I trust that all is in alignment with G-d's plan.

What I have come to know from Vahid's death is that we don't have to wait a lifetime to be whole. We don't have to wait from our deathbed to be whole. We don't have to wait for something exceptional to happen to forgive and let go. We can do it in the moment if we choose to.

This is the highest state of being—to be able to go forward in life with a sense of flow rather than brokenness and to be able to create our lives from that vantage point rather than from a place where all seems separated and unconnected.

We don't have to wait. The call of our lives is to allow the love to pour, to allow the walk to be with faith, to allow for growth to be with surrender, and to bless our moments with gratitude.

The sequoia tree is whole and complete in its entirety. Its roots are connected to the bark, which is connected to the branches, which are connected to the leaves. You might say, "Of course, it is. It is even ridiculous that you mention that." The roots are deep in the ground, with their network of being connected and intermingled with other roots. The bark is very tall, and yet there is a beautiful flow from the roots to the leaves. The roots look nothing like the branches and leaves. And yet there is a beautiful flow. Then how do we separate parts of our lives that seem to have nothing to do with one another?

Family
Friends
Community

We are here to evolve, to become, to be soulful, compassionate human beings.

U nder the ground all the way beneath the surface of the sequoia tree is a network of roots that are intertwined and interconnected. The roots of the sequoia trees within the grove or community make a complex web. The connection of the roots is what upholds the sequoia tree's gigantic size. The connection gives strength to the trees and serves as a network of communication among trees far grander than we can even imagine.

Never underestimate the power of family, friendship, and community. It is what held us in a cocoon of love. It is what embraced us in a web of compassion. It is what held us in times we fell. It is what gave Vahid strength and hope. I fully and completely believe that every single act of kindness, whether sent as a text or an actual visitation, became part of the light of his soul, and that is forever.

Vahid and I were blessed to be part of a family who gave selflessly, part of friendships that shared and cared endlessly, and part of a community that poured their love and support on our family.

The sequoia tree could never stand so tall had it not been for the roots that connect to one another and make a lattice of strength. They couldn't live for so long had it not been for the roots ever so patiently making their way to one another and becoming a bedrock of sustenance. This lattice is under the ground, hidden from sight, steeped all the way within the womb of the earth. It is from here, in this unseen depth, that the tree gets its nourishment from. It is from here, in the darkness of Mother Earth's womb, that the ingredients for growth come.

In a world where connection is regarded as getting you to places, the expression goes, "It's who you know, not what you know," and social climbing through these connections is a common theme. The connection that we are talking about here is inward, not outward. It's hidden, just like the roots of the sequoia tree. It acts for the sake of compassion, wants nothing back, except the connection itself, and desires to give of itself.

In Hebrew language, the word for *womb* is *rechem*, and the word for *compassion* is *rachamim*. It is in the womb of Mother Earth that not only germination but also sustenance takes place. The womb is hidden. It nourishes. It gives. It's patient. Its reward is the birth of life.

That's what connection is. Every time we give, we are birthing a new light within the person who is in pain. That birthing happens through compassion.

Compassion is being able to hold the person with love without impressing upon them our own personality. It's to be able to allow them to be without imposing on them how to be. It is to give them understanding for their situation and to be present for them. In that presence is where the sustenance lives.

Vahid's last year was shaped and formed by many factors, one of them being the love and compassion he received from others. Rather than becoming closed and shutting down because of his pain, his heart became more vibrant and effervescent. At times, you could see the love oozing out of him. It gave him the nourishment he needed for his soul to make it to another day.

We human beings are not meant to live our lives alone. The sequoia tree stands tall on its own. It has its own bark, branches, and leaves, and yet without the web that the roots create, none of that would be possible.

We are here to evolve, to become, to be soulful, compassionate human beings. However, that's impossible without the lattice and web of love. We would never be whole without our interconnectedness.

Pain and darkness are just as much part of life as joy and happiness, just like night is part of the day and winter is part of the seasons.

In an age where reason and logic prevail, there is nothing logical about pain and sadness. There could be no explanations for how one's journey unfolds, for no one really knows, except G-d. We live at a time where everyone has an explanation for everything, where our pain is a result of something we created from our conscious and subconscious, or so they say, where we get this pain to learn this lesson, where G-d is testing us, where life is hard and we have to fight for it, where we are not being the creators of our lives, or where we attract this to ourselves.

At times, I wanted to say "*Enough.*" We have to stop having explanations for everybody else's pain except ourselves. We have to stop dictating to others how to deal with grief and sadness. We have to remind ourselves that the person going through any tense situation needs nurturance and nourishment of the soul, not our opinion as to why their life is the way it is. We have to have compassion for the person going through any darkness, for they don't need to hear how that strengthens their soul and what strong people they will be as a result of their darkness.

They need compassion, which means they need to be heard, if they want to speak, without having our opinion imposed on them.

They need to be loved, without being told how to be.

They need to just be held and be given permission just to be, whether it's to cry or be alone.

Crying or being in pain is *not* a sign of weakness; it's a sign of our humanity.

We need to stop reasoning and start embracing our humanity.

Our humanity has all sorts of emotions and moves from one end of the spectrum to another. If we are not in pain, when someone close to us is suffering, then what can we be called? An enlightened human being? Far from it.

In an age where the pursuit of happiness has become the reason to be, we run away from pain, and we ask that anybody who is going through pain also not be in pain, because it's too hard for us to handle the darkness. Pain and darkness are just as much part of life as joy and happiness, just like night is part of the day and winter is part of the seasons. It's inevitable. If we don't fully embrace pain, then we can't fully embrace joy. It's part of the whole.

The sequoia tree in its magnificence doesn't justify the fire. It doesn't reason that because of this tree performing in this manner, it attracted the fire. It doesn't hold others responsible for the fire and ashes. If anything, the heat of the fire signals the tree to produce the fire retardant so it doesn't get consumed. It uses the roots to communicate to other trees that they too need to increase on their production of the fire retardant. It goes into action. It goes into supporting the other trees.

You think this is too far-fetched. Think again. There is plenty of research that shows that when trees are in distress, they send messages via their roots to either warn other trees or support them.

When there is hurt and pain, we need to have our fire retardant increased rather than reasoning why it's there. We need to support each other rather than offer our intellectual conclusion as to why that person is in pain.

I remember the first days that Vahid had started to feel really sick, and we were absolutely devastated. We could hardly do anything, and a sense of paralysis had taken over us. One of the greatest words of wisdom that

I heard, and it was extremely comforting to me, was from my wise cousin. She said, "I want you to know we are here with you. We are not leaving you alone or letting you go. We are all standing with you and behind you like soldiers. You have to tell us what you need, and we are right there for you. You are never alone. You will never be alone. We love you and Vahid dearly."

Then she gave me a hug that lasted minutes, and we cried together. That was beautiful. She didn't impose her opinion on how I should be or not be and didn't reason why my life has turned the way it has. She just gave me pure love and compassion. To this day, I hear her voice in my ears and appreciate the way she spoke to me as I had fallen.

Let our humanity be our humanity.

Let our tears be our tears.

Let our pain be our pain.

And then let love pour out from us toward the person in the dark.

Let compassion be our guiding light.

Let us embrace each other's pain as well as each other's joy.

Let us not reason someone else's pain.

Let us not bring logic into someone else's darkness.

Let us use our awareness not for deciphering G-dly knowledge, for it's out of our realm, but for shining our light and love into their weakened hearts.

The sequoia tree lets fire be fire, and then it grows. It lets ashes be ashes and then uses the ashes for germination. It lets the circumstances be as the circumstances, and it defies gravity.

Vahid also defied gravity. Even though he is no longer with us physically, he became the giant sequoia tree with his open heart, wisdom, and wholeness. He has shown us the germination of wisdom through ashes and the emergence of light through darkness. His love is with us every moment of every day with greater intensity than before. He, his essence, lives on and is continuing on the journey of light and wisdom.

I pray that no one goes through darkness. I pray that no one knows sadness like this. However, life is such that it evolves as it evolves. I pray that the unfoldment of our life is with unwavering faith, boundless love, surrender to the highest plan for us, and gratitude for all that is and has come to be.

I know this to be the truth, that G-d has given us the ability and capability, and I even go further than that, that it is our responsibility to become giants and masters of our lives and be sources of light, wisdom, strength, and support.

I know it to be true
that out of the ashes rises
the giant sequoia tree.

Credits

Rachel Shavolian for drawing the cover picture

Abner Zarabi for the picture on page x